Cheshire

David H. Pill

COUNTRYSIDE BOOKS
NEWBURY BERKSHIRE

First Published 2006
© David H. Pill, 2006

COUNTRYSIDE BOOKS
3 Catherine Road
Newbury, Berkshire

To view our complete range of books,
please visit us at
www.countrysidebooks.co.uk

ISBN 1 85306 970 1
EAN 978185306 970 3

*For Peter, to celebrate
an old friendship revived*

Cover picture shows the village of Caldy
Photographs by the author
Designed by Peter Davies, Nautilus Design
Produced through MRM Associates Ltd, Reading
Printed by Woolnough Bookbinding Ltd., Irthlingborough

Contents

Location map		4
Introduction		5

POCKET PUB WALKS

1	West Kirby (3¼ miles)	7
2	Willaston (6 miles)	12
3	Overton (3½ or 4 miles)	17
4	Sworton Heath (2¾ miles)	22
5	Dunham Woodhouses (5¼ miles)	27
6	Jackson's Bridge (3 or 6 miles)	32
7	Ollerton (4 miles)	37
8	Whiteley Green (4¾ miles)	42
9	Stamford Bridge (2¾ miles)	47
10	Eaton-by-Tarporley (3½ miles)	52
11	Goostrey (4 miles)	57
12	Sutton Lane Ends (3½ miles)	62
13	Astbury (4 miles)	67
14	Wybunbury (4 miles)	72
15	Grindley Brook (4½ miles)	77

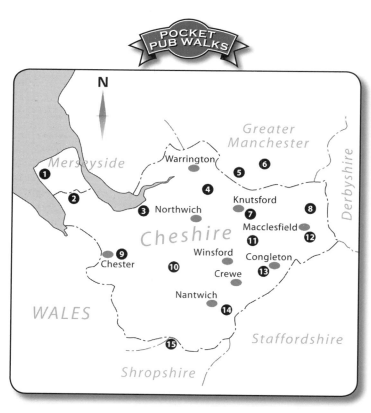

Area map showing location of the walks

Introduction

This is a book of walks in the old county of Cheshire, which, prior to the local government changes of 1974, included the whole of the Wirral peninsula and present-day Greater Manchester south of the Mersey. When most people think of Cheshire they will think of the great plain and its dairy farms, but almost everywhere we walk on that plain we can see the hills. To the west are the red sandstone hills, which we encounter above Frodsham, and to the east the gritstone hills of the Pennines, which we venture into near Macclesfield.

Wherever we go we can see how the geography of the county has shaped its history. There are hill-forts and castles, picturesque follies, Roman roads, canals and railways. Some of the latter are closed now, but, like the canal towpaths and many of the Roman roads, their former lines can be walked. Together with field-paths and lanes, they take us to the black and white, timbered manor houses for which the county is famous, to villages with greens and thatched cottages, to market town and mill town, and to fifteen excellent inns.

We visit seaside and countryside, woodland and pasture. We stroll along ancient sunken lanes to the sites of vanished manor houses, a lost village and a failed medieval borough. We see a rare floating bog and a beautiful valley with lakes where once there were gravel pits. There are rare breeds of sheep and cattle, shire horses and red deer, squirrels and rabbits, while both coast and country offer wonderful opportunities for bird-watchers. There are pub ghosts too and, very much alive, the invariably cheerful and helpful pub licensees. To them and their staff I owe a debt of gratitude for their time and their enthusiasm. Patrons will usually be able to leave their car in the pub car park while walking, but please seek permission first. Alternative parking suggestions are given, though.

I would like to thank my companions on these walks, Alan and Hilary Gent, Peter Mather, Michael and Wendy Rayner,

Elaine Sims and Paul Wood, for their help, advice and patience.

I hope you will enjoy these rambles in the lovely Cheshire countryside and the pub stops as much as I did. Happy walking!

David Pill

Publisher's Note

We hope that you obtain considerable enjoyment from this book; great care has been taken in its preparation. However, changes of landlord and actual closures are sadly not uncommon. Likewise, although at the time of publication all routes followed public rights of way or permitted paths, diversion orders can be made and permissions withdrawn.

We cannot, of course, be held responsible for such diversion orders and any inaccuracies in the text which result from these or any other changes to the routes nor any damage which might result from walkers trespassing on private property. We are anxious, though, that all details covering the walks and the pubs are kept up to date and would therefore welcome information from readers which would be relevant to future editions.

The simple sketch maps that accompany the walks in the book are based on notes made by the author whilst checking out the routes on the ground. For the benefit of a proper map, however, we do recommend that you purchase the relevant Ordnance Survey sheet covering your walk. The Ordnance Survey maps are widely available, especially through booksellers and local newsagents.

1 West Kirby

The Ring o' Bells

West Kirby has two sides to its character. There is the modern seaside town and, much less well known, the ancient village on the hill above it, which is the starting point for our walk. Here is the church that gives the place its name – Kirby means 'church town'. The 'West' distinguishes it from another Kirby a few miles to the east, the nucleus of the present-day Wallasey. We visit the church on our walk, but first it takes us across heathland with wonderful views over the Dee Estuary to North Wales, through National Trust woodland to the picture-postcard village of Caldy, and then along the Wirral Way. This former route of the Hooton to West Kirby railway, which closed in 1962, is England's oldest country park. We return to the car via a clifftop common and a public park with a profusion of roses in summer.

Distance – 3¼ miles.

OS Explorer 266 Wirral and Chester. GR 220863.

A long gradual climb at the start and one or two brief downhill stretches, otherwise level, easy walking.

Starting point The Ring o' Bells in West Kirby old village. Patrons may leave their cars in the pub car park while they walk – but please seek permission. Otherwise park carefully across the way in Devonshire Road.

How to get there The Ring o' Bells is on Village Road, just off the A540 between Hoylake and Heswall, ¾ mile east of West Kirby town centre. The walk is also accessible from West Kirby railway station via the Wirral Way.

THE PUB

The **Ring o' Bells** is a very comfortable pub developed from a former farmhouse built in 1810. In its spacious lounge, with pictures of old West Kirby on its walls, main courses such as slow-cooked Welsh lamb and pan fried spinach with a trio of mushrooms can be enjoyed. Light bites, which include crêpes, quiches and ploughman's lunches, are also available. Greene King, Morland Old Speckled Hen and the local brew, Cain's, are among the ales served.

Open from 11 am to 11.30 pm on Monday to Saturday and 12 noon to 11 pm on Sunday. Food is served from 12 noon to 10 pm every day.
☎ *0151 625 8103*

1 From the **Ring o' Bells** walk uphill along the road and take the third turning on the right, **Wetstone Lane**. Notice how the

sandstone walls here sometimes incorporate the bedrock. At the fork in the track pause to enjoy your first view of the **Dee** and the **Welsh hills**. Now continue uphill to the gate of **October House**.

2 Here bear right along a narrower path into a typical heathland wood of birch, oak and ash to emerge into an open area. Take the path on the right along a natural sandstone pavement. Here are two benches. From the first on a clear day you can see the mountains of **Snowdonia**, from the second the **Point of Ayr** at the end of the estuary, beyond it the **Great Orme** and to the right **Anglesey**. Continue along the sandstone pavement

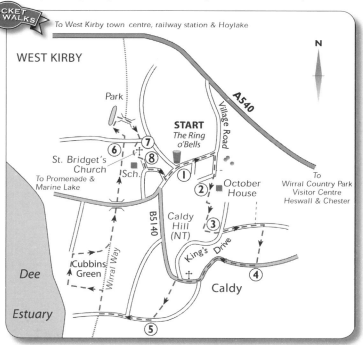

To West Kirby town centre, railway station & Hoylake

WEST KIRBY

N

Park

A540 Village Road

START
The Ring
o'Bells

6 **7**
St. Bridget's
Church
To Promenade &
Marine Lake
Sch.
8
1

2
October
House

To
Wirral Country Park
Visitor Centre
Heswall & Chester

B5140

Caldy
Hill
(NT)
3

King's Drive

Cubbins
Green

Wirral Way

4

Caldy

Dee

Estuary

5

and, beyond a third bench, fork right through the bracken. A little further on is a bench with a view over **West Kirby** and its marine lake to **Hilbre Island**. Continue ahead, ignoring the paths going downhill on the right. At a fork go left to pass a wall at right angles to you on the right. You are now in the National Trust property of **Caldy Hill**. Here there are more benches under the pine trees, this time with views upriver. Continue along the now wider main track to a T-junction of paths. Here pause to admire the impressive path through the rocks to the right and then go left to pass through a wall to a gate onto a road.

3 Go ahead along **King's Drive**, the West Kirby district's 'millionaire's row'. Look for footpaths to left and right. Take the one on the right, where, at the time of writing, there is a post but no sign. This is an ancient bridleway called **Fleck Lane**. There are steps in places, which are sometimes covered in leaves, so take care.

4 On reaching a road, cross to the pavement and turn right. You are now in the village of **Caldy**, which owes much of its picturesque appearance to the family of a Manchester merchant, Richard Barton, who bought it in the 1830s. You will pass their huge manor house on the right and then the mock-Tudor reading room and the church, which developed from a schoolroom they established for the village children. Turn right at the green to a cross erected to the memory of the last of his line, Alfred Barton, 'by many who loved him'. Now take the bridleway on the left, which narrows by the gate to a house. This path is sandy underfoot, making pleasant walking for tired feet, but watch out for tree roots.

5 At the end of the path turn right and walk down the road, keeping ahead at the junction and then turning right onto the **Wirral Way** by the remains of an old railway bridge. Take the path on the left to skirt the car park. Where the houses on the left end, turn left onto a path, which will take you onto a clifftop common called **Cubbins Green** or 'God's Little Acre'. Walk down the green and as you approach the houses do not go through the barrier but look for a grass track swinging right to regain the **Wirral Way** via a short flight of steps. Here turn left and continue.

6 After passing under the second bridge, turn left into the park. Keep the bowling green to your left and at the lake, go onto the higher footpath. Pass through a gap on the right, then turn right to cross a footbridge. Take the second of two paths immediately to your right. At the path's end, go half-right and, keeping the iron railing on your right, walk to the park exit.

7 Cross the road and go through the lychgate into the churchyard of **St Bridget's**. Walk on past the early 16th-century tower and, as you turn left, look for Queen Victoria's head on the south porch, a 19th-century addition. Head now towards the right-hand corner of the churchyard.

8 Pass through the gates, keeping the old school building on your right. Go left at the junction and left again to walk up through the village. Notice **Manor Farm** of 1665 to your left and, as you arrive back at the car park, the ancient cottage with the lucky black cat in its thatch to your right.

Place of interest nearby

The **Wirral Country Park Visitor Centre** is at Thurstaston, about 3¾ miles south-east of the Ring o' Bells and reached by turning right (south-west) at the Cottage Loaf pub. It contains exhibits relating to the history of the former railway, whose station platforms survive close by, and to the flora and fauna of the Wirral Way. There is a bird hide with information on what to look for, also picnic tables and a café, while steps lead down to a sandy beach. Open 10 am to 5 pm every day except Christmas Day.
☎ 0151 648 4371

 **Willaston**

The Nag's Head

Willaston was, it is said, the ancient capital of Wirral, the peninsula's name being derived from that of the village. The representatives of the villages in the Willaston or Wirral Hundred are thought to have met on Willaston's green. It is still there, overlooked by some of the lovely old houses for which the village is noted. We see a number of these on our walk, which takes us to a disused but preserved railway station, the site of a lost village, three garden centres all in a row, a riding school, a secret garden and an old pumping station which looks like a church, all set in a delightful pastoral landscape.

12

THE PUB

The **Nag's Head**, which looks onto the green, was built in 1733, although it has been much altered since. A comfortable pub with a separate dining area, it serves Tetley's ales and Carlsberg lager plus two different guest beers each week. The food on the specials board also varies from week to week, but may include such tempting dishes as lamb steak in red wine and rosemary and Mediterranean salmon. Permanently on the menu are home-made curries, steak and kidney pie, a ploughman's lunch and various sandwiches, toasties and jacket potatoes.

Open from 12 noon to 11 pm on Monday to Saturday and 12 noon to 10.30 pm on Sunday. Food is served from 12 noon to 7.30 pm on Monday to Saturday and 12 noon to 6.30 pm on Sunday.
☎ *0151 327 2439*

Distance – 6 miles.

OS Explorer 266 Wirral and Chester. GR 330777.

A level walk down quiet lanes, across fields and along the Wirral Way.

Starting point The Nag's Head in Willaston. Patrons may leave their cars in the pub car park while they walk – but please seek permission. Otherwise park on the village green. Alternatively, you could start the walk at Hooton railway station, point 7.

How to get there *The Nag's Head, which is on the B5133, is situated 2½ miles west of junction 5 of the M53 and 1½ miles east of the A540 Hoylake to Chester road.*

Cheshire

1 Turn right out of the **Nag's Head car park** and on reaching the green, cross into **Hadlow Road**. The timbered building to your right is the former **Red Lion inn**, dating from 1631. The venerable building you are approaching on the left is the **Old Hall**, which bears the date 1558. Further down the road you will pass a farmhouse of 1739 on your right and then on the left the picturesque **Ash Tree Farm**.

2 On reaching the former level crossing look left and you will see the preserved **Hadlow Road station** on the **Wirral Way**, at which you may wish to take a closer look. To continue the walk, go over the crossing and turn down the lane to your left. After passing a farm on the left, look for a stile on the right. Cross it and walk along the left-hand side of a hedge to a further stile and a plank bridge. Turn right into the lane and, when level

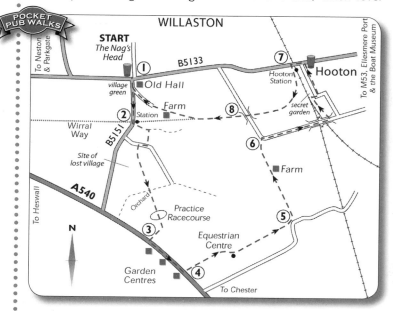

with a pylon, look for another plank bridge and stile to your left. Cross these and walk down the right-hand edge of the field. This and adjacent fields are believed to be the site of the lost Domesday village of **Hadlow**. Cross a further stile and go ahead, aiming to the left of the bungalow. Cross the drive and walk between a fence and woodland to cross another drive and follow a wall on your right past an orchard to another stile. Go over the racehorse practice track and cross the meadow to a stile by a warning sign. Cross

The imposing old pumping station at Hooton.

it and walk down the left-hand edge of another meadow to a plank bridge. Cross this and a stile and turn right. Walk along the edge of the field to a stile hidden in a hawthorn hedge to gain access to the main road.

3 Turn left and walk along the pavement until you come to a kissing gate in the hedge to your left.

4 Through the gate you will come to a fence, which, at the time of writing, lacks a stile. Beyond it, walk along the right-hand side of the field to a further fence. On the other side, cross a track to a stile and again walk along the right-hand side of the field. If there is a crop growing in the next field, the footpath may be difficult to find; nevertheless there is a right of way here. You will eventually reach a gate onto a track through an equestrian centre. The track then becomes a made-up lane.

5 At the end of the lane you will pass over a cattle grid to a road junction. Here turn left into the drive to **Oaks Farm**, with its avenue of oaks and well-kept verges.

6 Leaving the farm and its fields behind, go through a gate and at the road junction turn right into the perfect country lane. Cross two railway bridges. Immediately after the second bridge, go down some steps on the left to a narrow path alongside the railway. The path turns right and on the left you will see a stream and a charming wayside garden where you may wish to rest awhile. Now turn left into a lane. Having passed the old **pumphouse** and **Hooton station car park** you will come to the **Hooton Hotel**.

7 Turn left onto the main road, cross the railway bridge and, at the **Wirral Way** sign, go down the slope on the left. Soon you are walking on the former platform of the West Kirby branch line.

8 Pass under a bridge and turn very briefly right into a lane and then left onto a path by a gate (parallel to but to the right of the **Wirral Way**). The path becomes a bridleway between high hedges and then a farm track. The track becomes a made-up but rough lane as you re-enter **Willaston village**. On reaching the main road, turn right to return to the **Nag's Head**.

Place of interest nearby

Sited where the Shropshire Union Canal joined the Mersey, and easily reached from Willaston via the M53, the **Boat Museum at Ellesmere Port** offers you the opportunity to explore 7½ acres of canal warehousing and workers' cottages. You can hop aboard the narrowboats and even take a journey along the canal. There are also excellent views over the Manchester Ship Canal and the river. Open every day in summer, 10 am to 5 pm, and from Wednesday to Saturday in winter, 11 am to 4 pm.
☎ 0151 355 5017

3 Overton

The Ring o' Bells

Overton is situated, as its name might suggest, on a hillside above the market town of Frodsham. Here, close to some picturesque old houses and cottages, is the church of St Laurence. Externally 14th- and 15th-century, it has an impressive Norman nave. From the church we walk through the woods along an ancient sunken lane to the hamlet of Bradley and then along more lanes and field-paths with wonderful views over the Weaver valley, the Cheshire plain, the Mersey estuary and Frodsham itself. On our way we visit some mysterious caves. It is believed by some local historians that they were formed by quarrying for building sand in Georgian days. However, pottery from Civil War times found in their vicinity suggests that people were living or hiding there a century earlier.

Distance – 3½ or 4 miles.

OS Explorer 267 Northwich and Delamere Forest. GR 521772.

The walk does involve some climbing and there are some tricky steps to negotiate at one point, though an alternative route is provided. However, most reasonably fit people will have little difficulty in completing it.

Starting point The Ring o' Bells in Bellemonte Road, Overton. The pub car park is available for patrons while they walk, but please ask first. Otherwise leave your car in the car park by St Laurence's church, which is used by pub customers, churchgoers and the general public.

How to get there The Ring o' Bells is about ¾ mile from Frodsham town centre via Church Road/Howey Lane, which links the B5152 to Delamere and Tarporley with the A56 to Helsby and Chester. Turn off south into Bellemonte Road opposite the church. There is a railway station at Frodsham on the Warrington to Chester line.

THE PUB

The **Ring o' Bells** is a charming old place with small rooms, low-beamed ceilings and a pleasant garden. Built in Tudor times it has been an inn since at least 1666. Theakston's is always on draught and there are guest beers, while the menu includes steak and Guinness pie, plaice stuffed with prawns and mushrooms, Cumberland sausage and mash, smoked salmon and asparagus quiche, and deep-fried Camembert and cranberry salad. There are also sandwiches and toasties, which can be enjoyed by a roaring fire in winter.

Open from 12 noon to 3 pm and 5.30 pm to 11 pm on Monday to Friday, 12 noon to 4 pm and 6 pm to 11 pm on Saturday and 12 noon to 4 pm and 7 pm to 11 pm on Sunday. Food is served every day from 12 noon to 2 pm and at other times by prior arrangement.
☎ *01928 732068*

1. From the **Ring o' Bells** turn right into **Church Road** and walk past the church to its end. Cross the main road, with care, to enter **Townfield Lane**.

2. Where the houses end on the right and the lane narrows, look for a public footpath sign. Turn into the path, from which, before it becomes high-hedged, there are views of the **Weaver valley**. Where the path forks, carry on ahead along what becomes a sunken lane over-arched with trees. Ignore the footpath up the steps to the left and drop down through the woods to a bridge over a stream. There is a picnic area to the left just after the bridge. Carry on ahead to emerge from the wood onto a hedged path with cobbles under the grass. There is now a wider view over the **Weaver valley** to the left. At the barn conversion (**Dingle Barn**) go right. This is **Bradley**.

3. At the crossroads go ahead into pleasant, quiet **Watery Lane**. Ignore footpaths to right and left and go down the dip in the lane to cross a stream by an 18th-century farmhouse. Continue up the rise and go right at the junction, following the main route of the lane. You will find lots of elderberries here in their season.

4. Look for a footpath sign on the left and walk up the field on a well-defined path. If you turn round, you will see a superb view. There is **Fiddler's Ferry power station** on the banks of the Mersey, the impressive sandstone water tower at **Norton** near Runcorn and the white concrete tower of the nuclear research laboratories at

Cheshire

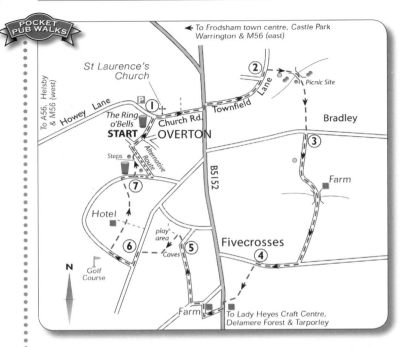

Daresbury, and further right a wonderful view across the Cheshire plain to the **Pennines**. Pass the gate of the house on the left and look for a stone stile amongst the bracken. Go briefly left along the roadside pavement and then right into a lane. Walk uphill, passing **Such Farm**, and follow the road round to the right. At the junction, with its small green, keep left and then turn right into **Top Road.**

5 Where the road bends to the right, cross a small ladder stile by a sandstone cottage and walk towards the children's playground, looking for a stile on the left. Cross this and walk uphill. There may be cattle here so if you have a dog please keep it on its lead. Cross the stile at the top of the hill and go right, taking the lower of two paths. Having walked through the gorse, look

out for the caves on your left, then continue downhill.

6 Cross the small ladder stile and turn left to walk along the road, turning right by the junction. Passing the entrance to a golf club on your left, turn right at the gate to **Overhill Cottage**. Where the drive swings towards the cottage (actually a bungalow) keep ahead on a mown path. On the left in the trees is the **Heathercliffe Hotel**, long the hideaway of celebrities visiting the North West. It is open to non-residents so you might like to investigate further. Otherwise cross the hotel drive onto a downhill path. On reaching a lane, turn right.

7 Unless you have difficulty with steps, turn left at the **Belle Monte Hotel** and take the path on the right. This will immediately fork and you should take the paved path along the right-hand edge of the wood. Take care on the steps, particularly after the leaves have fallen. (An alternative route is to follow the road round to the right at the **Belle Monte** and continue along it as it swings left. This way is about ½ mile longer but you will be rewarded with a splendid view of **the Mersey Estuary**.) At the foot of the steps, go ahead down the road. At the junction look right and you will see a very quaint timber-framed cottage. Now walk on past the **Bull's Head** to the **Ring o' Bells** and the car park.

Place of interest nearby

The **Lady Heyes Crafts and Antiques Centre** offers another amazing view. To see it, drive 1½ miles down the B5152 towards Delamere and you will find the centre on the left. In addition to the view, there are galleries selling individually crafted gifts, craft supplies, books, records, pictures, antiques and collectables, as well as an award-winning tearoom and restaurant and a play barn for the children.
☎ 01928 787919

4 Sworton Heath

The Bear's Paw

Sworton Heath is the starting point for a walk that will appeal to those who like the wide open spaces. It takes us across the former heaths and mosses and along the country lanes of north Cheshire and provides us with some splendid views. It also enables us to take a look at one of the county's oldest houses, Swineyard Hall. There was certainly a house on the site in the 14th century, but the discovery of a Stone Age axe-hammer suggests that it may have been occupied very much earlier.

THE PUB The welcoming **Bear's Paw** is a 17th-century former farmhouse which has been a pub for about 80 years. Small-roomed and cosy inside, with a restaurant, it has an attractive and extensive beer garden with a children's play area. It serves John Smith's, Thwaite's and Marston's ales. From the main

Distance – 2¾ miles.

OS Explorer 276 Bolton, Wigan and Warrington.
GR 689842.

Although there are one or two slight gradients, on the whole this is level, easy walking suitable for all the family.

Starting point The Bear's Paw in Sworton Heath. Please seek the licensee's permission if you want to leave your car in the pub car park while walking.

How to get there The Bear's Paw is on the A50 Warrington to Macclesfield road 2 miles east of junction 20 on the M6.

menu, one can order generous servings of lamb and rosemary and Scottish salmon and crayfish, while those who prefer smaller meals can enjoy lamb cutlets, ham and eggs, scampi or cod. On the snacks menu are various salads, sandwiches and wraps, while the home-made desserts include the house speciality, ticky-tacky pudding.

Open from 11.30 am to 11 pm on Monday to Saturday and 12 noon to 10.30 pm on Sunday. Food is served from 12 noon to 2 pm every weekday, 6 pm to 9 pm on Tuesday to Saturday and 12 noon to 4 pm on Sunday, when it is advisable to book.
☎ *01925 752573*

1 From the **Bear's Paw** cross the main road, with care, to a lane opposite the car park exit. Walk past a timber-framed cottage with brick nogging, onto what becomes a dirt track with tennis courts on the right and a tree nursery across the field to the left. You may see or hear pheasants as you cross a stile into a

big field, where you should head to the right of a dilapidated barn. (In wet conditions or if the hay has not been mown, it is advisable to take a longer route round the right-hand edge of the field.) Having passed the barn, walk along the right-hand side of a row of oaks and a hawthorn hedge, where you will hear the ripple of water from a hidden stream. Go ahead at a stile onto a green track with a hawthorn hedge to the right. The large farm ahead is called **Moss Hall**, for all this now dry land was once moss land. You are likely to see rabbits scurrying around in this apparently abandoned field. At its end carry on along a track, passing a pond on the right and a green barn on the left.

2 Turn right onto a lane with a verge. There is a ditch or stream on the right where hogweed and cow parsley grow. At the

Swineyard Hall is surrounded by a moat.

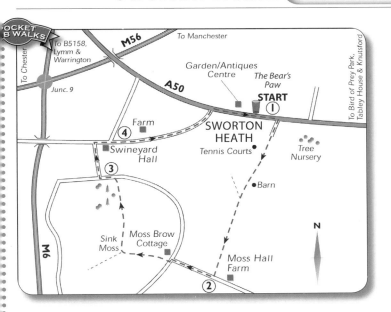

end of the lane have a look at the white house called **Moss Brow**, which is dated 1749 and has an old pump and well-head in its garden. Now cross the stile to its left to walk between garden and hedge to another stile. Beyond it, walk the wide path that a thoughtful farmer has left between his crops. This rich farmland was once the ominously named **Sink Moss**. There are wide views of both farmland and woodland to be enjoyed from here. At the footpath sign, turn right to follow the left-hand edge of the same field, taking care not to damage the crop. The official path runs along the ridge to your left but this is so overgrown as to be impassable. Again there are wonderfully wide views. Looking right you may be able to see **Cage Hill** with its tower in National Trust owned **Lyme Park**. The building on the rise ahead is **Swineyard Hall**. Walk along the edge of the pine wood to reach **Moss Lane**, where you should turn left.

Cheshire

3 Walk the brief distance to the junction and turn right into **Moss Brow Lane**. Enjoy another good view before a high hawthorn hedge obscures it. If you are here in early autumn, you may wish to pick some blackberries on this quiet lane before you turn right into one where you may meet some traffic. Please take special care on the bends. Having turned the corner, look to the right and you will see the front garden of **Swineyard Hall** and its moat. The oldest part of the existing building is on the left and is probably 16th-century.

4 Go straight ahead at the road junction and enjoy the views over the cornfields. The presence of bracken here betrays the fact that this was once heathland as does the name of **Sworton Heath Farm** on the left. This is a traditional old Cheshire farmhouse, many of which have been replaced in recent years. Cheshire potatoes may be growing in some of the fields further along the lane, while the neglected ones have been colonised by willowherb, bindweed and rabbits. At the lane's end, cross the main road with care and turn right to walk along the pavement to the **Bear's Paw**, noticing the old farm cart by its former barn, where garden furniture and antiques are now sold.

Place of interest nearby

Gauntlet Bird of Prey and Vulture Park houses more then ninety birds of prey from the world's smallest owls to its largest eagles and is also the largest falconry centre in the North West. Open every afternoon, there is a flying display at 3 pm. The centre offers courses in falconry and avian photography, while next door there is a well-stocked garden centre with an excellent café. It is situated alongside the A50 on the outskirts of Knutsford, 4½ miles from the Bear's Paw.
☎ *01565 754419*

5 Dunham Woodhouses

The Vine

Dunham Woodhouses is an estate village attached to **Dunham Massey,** a National Trust property that was once the home of the Earls of Stamford and Warrington. From here our walk, which will have a special appeal to those interested in transport history, follows the towpath of the Bridgewater Canal. This was designed by James Brindley and opened in 1776 to link Manchester and its cotton industry with the Mersey at Runcorn, and the port of Liverpool. We then walk a field-path to the village of Heatley, where we join the Trans Pennine Trail, which makes use here of the Garston (Liverpool) to Timperley (Altrincham) railway route. The line was opened in 1853 and carried passenger traffic until 1962 and goods until 1985.

THE PUB

The **Vine** does not attract attention to itself. It is hidden away off the village street and is easily missed, but it is worth seeking out. In its small rooms are served some excellent home-cooked meals, among them home-made pies – including cheese and onion, corned beef and potato and steak and ale – home-made curries, of which beef Madras seems to be particularly popular, a daily roast and an all-day breakfast. Sandwiches are also available and can be washed down with a pint of John Smith's.

Open from 11 am to 11 pm on Monday to Saturday and 12 noon to 10.30 pm on Sunday. Food is served from 12 noon to 2 pm and 5.30 pm to 8.30 pm on Monday to Saturday and 12 noon to 5 pm on Sunday.
☎ *0161 928 3275*

Distance – 5¼ miles.

OS Explorer 276 Bolton, Wigan and Warrington.
GR 724879.

Easy, level walking, which, punctuated by stops for refreshment, can be enjoyed by all the family.

Starting point The Vine pub in Dunham Woodhouses. Patrons may use the Vine's car park while they walk – but please seek permission first. Otherwise there are parking places just beyond the canal bridge and you should start the walk at point 2.

How to get there *The Vine is on the west side of the B5160 Warburton to Altrincham road 1½ miles south-east of the A6144 and 2 miles north-west of the A56. It is easily reached via the latter road from junction 7 of the M56.*

A family of swans on the Bridgewater canal.

1 From the **Vine car park** cross to the pavement on the other side of the road and turn right. Follow the road round to the left and again cross to the pavement. There are some very attractive old cottages along this lane, one on the right having a particularly delightful cottage garden.

2 Just before the canal bridge turn right, follow the track onto the towpath and bear right along it. Where you cross the aqueduct over the **river Bollin** the tall building to your left is a former watermill. Further left can be seen the wall round **Dunham Massey's park** and its early 18th-century stables. Passing under the first bridge, notice the old crane to the left. Further along the tower of **Warburton church**, designed by John Douglas, who provided Chester with some of its most notable mock-Tudor buildings, can be seen to your right with **Winter Hill** in the background. Should you be in need of refreshment as you pass the **Barn Owl pub**, which stands tantalisingly on the opposite bank, ring the bell and someone should appear to row you across.

Having passed an old canal warehouse and crossed a bridge over a lane you will see the prominent spire of **Oughtrington church**, whose Victorian chancel is said to be an exact replica of the chancel of Westminster Abbey. The new woodland across

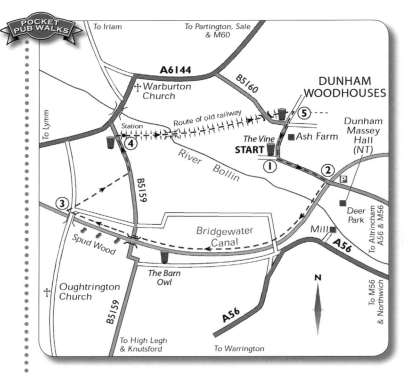

the canal was planted to commemorate the millennium and the local children were allowed to decide its name. They chose to call it **Spud Wood**.

3 Leave the canal at the next bridge, immediately below the church. This is called **Lloyd Bridge** after a family who worked on the canal for nearly two hundred years. Walk ahead down the lane and go across the junction onto a narrow path alongside an electricity substation. Carry on across the field and then walk along the right-hand side of the hedge to emerge onto a lane at a kissing gate. Turn left and walk up the lane to the **Railway**

Hotel in **Heatley**, where there are railway pictures on the walls and a notable collection of beer mats.

Turn right onto the old railway track, passing the former **Heatley station** and its platform on your left. In early summer you will enjoy the scent of may blossom and of bluebells as you approach the viaduct over the **Bollin**. Here you will learn that you are 47½ miles from Southport and 166 from Hornsea at either end of the **Trans Pennine Trail**. Further along is an interpretation board with a picture of the railway in its heyday. You will find lots of broom in the next section and, having crossed a track, enter a cutting that, in season, is blue with forget-me-nots. Pass under the bridge and turn right onto the lane by the stationmaster's house of the former **Dunham Massey station**.

Walk down the lane to the **Rope and Anchor** and perhaps enjoy a pint of John Smith's, Marston's Pedigree or Deuchar's on the bench outside the pub. You may prefer to carry on ahead at the junction and call in at **Ash Farm** for some of its delicious home-made ice-cream. Continue down the lane, looking out on the left for the early 18th-century **Manor Farm**, whose fine wrought iron railings incorporate the cipher of the second Earl of Warrington. Opposite this is a house of 1752 with elaborate gate piers. Just beyond it turn right into the **Vine's car park**.

Place of interest nearby

Dunham Massey is a must while you are in the area. In addition to the magnificent Georgian mansion, its beautiful garden and its deer park, there is a working, 17th-century, water-powered sawmill. The park is open every day from 9 am and the house from March to October every day except Thursday and Friday from 12 noon to 5 pm.
☎ *0161 941 4351*

The Jackson's Boat

Jackson's Bridge crosses the river Mersey near the town of Sale. This part of the Mersey valley is an amazing green oasis in the midst of one of the most highly populated areas in the Greater Manchester conurbation. In recent years it has been much enhanced by tree planting and the conversion of two pits, excavated to provide gravel and sand for building the embankment carrying the M63 (now M60) motorway, into lakes for water sports and fishing. We visit both of these, two nature reserves and a new area of woodland, and walk beside the river and down a lane, where, surprisingly, there are still working farms.

THE PUB The **Jackson's Boat** takes its name from someone who used to ferry people across the river before it was bridged at this point. Despite its proximity to the M60 it is hidden away in a peaceful, wooded spot and has a pleasant garden and a

Distance – 6 miles (or two walks, each of 3 miles).

OS Explorer 277 Manchester and Salford. GR 810926.

Level, easy walking, but be prepared for muddy patches on the footpaths, especially after rain.

Starting point The Jackson's Boat pub. Customers, having asked the landlord's permission, may leave their cars in the pub car park while they walk. Alternatively, park at the Mersey Valley Visitor Centre, on the lane going left off the one to the pub, and start the walk at point 2. The walk route (point 5) can also be reached by walking along the canal towpath from Stretford Metro-link station.

How to get there *The Jackson's Boat is at the end of a lane running north-east, away from Sale town centre, from junction 6 of the M60 Manchester orbital road.*

children's play area. It serves good quality, traditional pub food, including steak and Old Speckled Hen pie, sausage and mash, and haddock, chips and mushy peas. Vegetarian meals and sandwiches are also available. Ales on draught include Morland Old Speckled Hen, Bateman's XXXB and Timothy Taylor's Landlord. The early 18th-century building and its conservatory-like extension are kept spotlessly clean, and walkers, though welcome, are asked to leave their muddy boots outside.

Open from 11 am to 11 pm on Monday to Saturday and 12 noon to 10.30 pm on Sunday. Food is served from 12 noon to 9 pm on Monday to Saturday and 12 noon to 7 pm on Sunday.
☎ *0161 905 2647*

1 Walk to the far left-hand corner of the pub car park and exit it onto a track. Beyond the gate, bear left and walk along an avenue of young oaks. You will soon be on an embankment where you should keep left and go through a gate by a board listing the benefits of walking. Ignore the paths to left and right and walk alongside the road to the visitor centre.

2 After looking at the wildflower bank to the centre's right and reading the interpretation board, bear right down the steps and then go ahead over a crosspath. Go through the barrier and turn right onto a lane. You will pass a wetlands viewing platform on the right. Continue along the lane to **Sale Water Park**.

3 Pause for a while to enjoy the view across the lake with its swans and Canada geese towards the **Trafford Water Sports Centre**. Now continue along the lane past two islands with an assault course. Go through the gate and look out on the right for a bird hide from which to view the **Broad Ees Dole Nature Reserve** with its waders and warblers.

4 At the end of the lake fork right and cross the bridge over the **Mersey**. Walk ahead alongside the railway embankment, which now carries the **Metro-link tramway** from Altrincham to Manchester city centre.

5 Follow the track under the tramway and then under a bridge carrying the **Bridgewater Canal**. Turn immediately right and go through a gap in the fence. It is a tight squeeze and you may find it easier to look for a way off the track a little further up. Turn right and walk along the lane, passing **Stretford Cemetery** on your left. Do not turn left onto the grassland but carry on until you reach a dry weir. Go ahead here, ignoring the lane to your left and the steps up the embankment on your right. Pass some sports fields on your left and turn right to cross a bridge over the **Chorlton Brook**.

6 Turn left into the **Chorlton Ees Nature Reserve** and follow the brook along a tree-lined avenue. Cross a car park onto a cobbled track and turn right by the **Trans Pennine Trail** sign onto a track that is initially paved with setts. Pass through a wetland area with a meadow to the left. Continue ahead to the riverbank. As you pass the river overflow you will see **Jackson's Bridge** ahead. You may, if you wish, shorten the walk by crossing the bridge back to the pub.

7 If you have decided to carry on, walk on beside the river, passing **Chorlton golf course** and then going down the slope into **Chorlton**

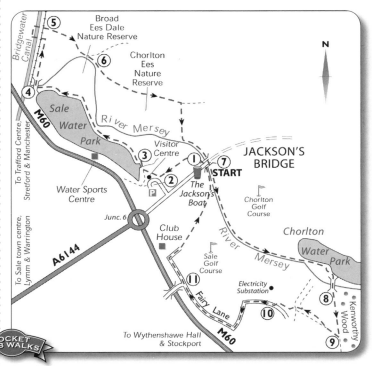

Water Park. Turn right alongside the lake. When you reach the 'access for all' garden with its plants to see, touch and smell to your right, take the path closer to the water by the 'No fishing, no swimming' sign. At its end, cross the bridge over the river.

8 Walk up the lane ahead. To your left is **Kenworthy Wood**. Pass the entrance to a wildflower meadow on your right and walk on until you reach the overhead cables.

9 Turn right onto a track, which follows the pylons. An alternative is to look for a gap in a fence on the right and follow a parallel track, passing some silver-leaved poplars to your right. Where this track swings right, climb up the bank ahead, turn left onto another track and go downhill towards the electricity substation.

10 Here enter **Fairy Lane**. Pass a smallholding on your left and then follow the lane left and right past a riding school, a boarding kennels and a farm with some unusual cattle.

11 Do not cross the motorway but keep ahead towards **Sale Golf Club** and then turn right onto a path alongside the golf course. At its end, keep ahead alongside the river to return to the **Jackson's Boat**.

Place of interest nearby

Wythenshawe Hall, signposted from the A5103, ½ mile south of junction 5 of the M60, is a 16th-century timber-framed house with a notable collection of furniture and pictures. In its 270 acre park are pitch and putt and crazy golf courses and a pets corner. Pony rides are available if booked in advance. Open from Easter to September, 10 am to 5 pm on Thursday to Sunday and bank holidays.
☎ *0161 998 2331*

7 Ollerton

The Dun Cow

Ollerton must seem to most people driving along the **A537** to be simply a few houses around a crossroads. This walk takes us into the hidden village, a delightful place of picture-postcard cottages and handsome old houses, and then across fields hedged about with wildflowers for much of the year and through areas of largely deciduous woodland.

THE PUB The **Dun Cow** was once the village's courthouse as well as its inn. Today it is a smart well-kept hostelry with charming staff. It serves ale brewed at the Weetwood Brewery in Tarporley as well as a drink that once virtually monopolised the area and is now rarely found here, Greenalls Bitter. The menu, which features old favourites such as ham and eggs, pork chops and beef salad, is changed every couple of days, and special two course lunches are offered from Monday to Thursday. Sandwiches, such as ham and mustard and Cheddar cheese with onion relish, served with salad and chips, are available up to 4 pm.

Open from 12 noon to 11 pm on Monday to Saturday and 12 noon to 10.30 pm on Sunday. Food is served from 12 noon to 9.30 pm on Monday to Saturday and 12 noon to 8.30 pm on Sunday.
☎ 01565 633093.

1 From the **Dun Cow car park** turn left to walk on the pavement alongside the A537. This is a comparatively quiet main road and provides quite pleasant walking. There is a tall beech hedge on the left and then a gate, where it is worth pausing to enjoy a view over a parkland-like pastoral landscape. Go ahead at the crossroads, noticing the gazebo at wisteria-clad **Ollerton House**.

2 On reaching a farm, cross over the road and enter **School Lane**. Pass elegant **Sycamore Farm House** with its coat of arms on

Distance – 4 miles.

OS Explorer 268 Wilmslow, Macclesfield and Congleton. GR 774769.

An easy walk over level ground, suitable for all.

Starting point The Dun Cow in Ollerton. The pub car park is available for customers while they are walking, but please ask the manager for permission first.

How to get there *The Dun Cow is 1½ miles south-east of Knutsford town centre on the A537 Macclesfield road.*

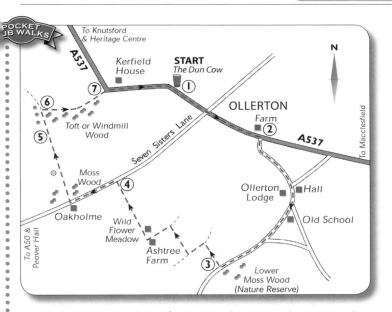

To Knutsford
& Heritage Centre

A537

Kerfield
House

START
The Dun Cow

(1)

N

OLLERTON

Farm
(2)

A537

To Macclesfield

(7)

(6)

Toft or Windmill
Wood

(5)

Seven Sisters Lane

Moss
Wood

(4)

Ollerton
Lodge

Hall

Old School

Oakholme

Wild
Flower
Meadow

Ashtree
Farm

(3)

Lower
Moss Wood
(Nature Reserve)

To A50 &
Peover Hall

POCKET
JB WALKS

your left and then a line of attractive houses and cottages. One thatched cottage has an unusual oriel window. Look left at the junction to see the early 18th-century façade of the largely 16th-century **Ollerton Hall** and then continue ahead, passing the **Old Stables** on the left and more former stables, now **Stable Cottage**, on the right. These belonged to **Ollerton Lodge**, whose cobbled yard you now see. The prominent Hanoverian royal arms are said to have come from a mill owned by a family who once lived here. The Lodge itself is a lovely bay-windowed Georgian house. By the small green you will see the building that was the village school from 1876 until 1994. Carry on ahead as the pavement gives way to a verge. Look out on the right for timber-framed **Oak Farm House** at the end of its yard. At the next junction again go forward. On the left is **Lower Moss Wood Educational Nature Reserve** with its wildlife hospital. If you wish to visit it you should telephone 01565 735082 in advance.

3 Where the wooded area on the right ends turn right onto a bridleway through dairy pasture. Follow the track to left and then right. The farmer has left a large border for wildflowers to grow between the path and his crop; red poppies stand out amongst a white mass of scented mayweed in summer. The track will bend left to a footpath

The imposing Kerfield House, Ollerton.

sign. Ignore this and stay on the bridleway, heading for the farm. Here go slightly right to pass between farm buildings to reach the front of the house and then bear right onto a tarmac drive. In season, enjoy the wildflower meadow on your left as you head for a lane.

4 On reaching it turn left and take care as the traffic seems to speed along here. At a house called **Oakholme** turn right and cross a stile into **Moss Wood**. Keep ahead through this quiet beech and birch woodland to another stile and continue along the left-hand edge of the field, passing a pond on your left. The area around the next stile is overgrown so go through the gate where the path becomes more of a green lane. As you tread cones from a solitary pine tree you may see, above the trees ahead, planes coming in to land at Manchester Airport.

5 At the next field the path narrows. On reaching a broken stile go ahead into **Windmill** or **Toft Wood**, a largely deciduous woodland with some conifers and an underplanting of rhododendrons. Cross the ditch and take care to stay on the path; this part of the wood is quite swampy and there may be shooting going on.

6 When you reach a point where fields can be seen to your right, turn sharp right over a (probably) dry ditch and keep the fields to your left. There are some splendid beech trees and then what amounts to an avenue of trees with oaks conspicuous amongst them.

7 At the main road, cross over to the pavement and turn right. The imposing **Kerfield House** on your left is not what it seems. Its convincing 'Georgian' façade was designed by Sir Percy Worthington and added to what is basically a Victorian house in 1912. Having admired it, continue along the pavement to the **Dun Cow**.

Places of interest nearby

Knutsford Heritage Centre in King Street is housed in a 17th-century former smithy and has a changing range of exhibitions on local history, crafts, conservation and other topics, as well as a permanent exhibition 'The Story of Knutsford' (Mrs Gaskell's *Cranford*). There is also a shop selling environmentally friendly gifts. Open 1.30 pm to 4 pm on Monday to Friday and 11 am to 4 pm on Sunday.
☎ *01565 605506*

Peover Hall, about 4 miles from the Dun Cow and reached via Seven Sisters Lane, the A50 and the village of Over Peover, was the wartime headquarters of General George S. Patton and the US 3rd Army. The Hall, whose most impressive feature is its huge kitchen, was built in 1585. It is open on Mondays, except bank holidays, between May and September from 2 pm to 4.30 pm, while its gardens and 17th-century stables can be viewed on Thursdays from 2 pm to 5 pm.
☎ *01565 750151*

8 Whiteley Green

The Windmill

Whiteley Green is in the parish of Adlington** but our walk takes us into the neighbouring parishes of Poynton and Pott Shrigley. First we use the Middlewood Way, the route of the Macclesfield to Marple railway, which was opened in 1869 and closed in 1970. Then we join the towpath of the Macclesfield Canal. The last waterway of the canal age, completed in 1831, it linked the Trent and Mersey and Peak Forest canals. We then walk along footpaths and lanes to see a secret cottage in the woods and a very curious tearoom and over a hill with a superb view.

 THE PUB The **Windmill**, an inn since 1784, is a pub restaurant serving a variety of ales: Morland Old Speckled Hen, Timothy Taylor's, Black Sheep and Tetley's. Its meals, cooked from fresh produce, have a real flavour of the North West about them.

Bury black pudding and Morecambe Bay shrimps are amongst the starters. Main courses, which are served with imaginatively prepared vegetables, include Heathcote's bangers (from a local butcher), rib-eye of Adlington beef, roast rack of Lune valley lamb and gateau of Nantwich goat's cheese, aubergines and plum tomatoes. Cheshire farm ice-creams and Lancashire and Cheshire cheeses feature on the desserts menu.

Open from 12 noon to 3 pm and 5 pm to 11 pm on Monday to Friday, 12 noon to 11 pm on Saturday and 12 noon to 10.30 pm on Sunday. Food is served from 12 noon to 2.30 pm on Monday to Friday, 12 noon to 9 pm on Saturday and 12 noon to 7.30 pm on Sunday.
☎ *01625 574222*

Distance – 4¾ miles.

OS Explorer 268 Wilmslow, Macclesfield and Congleton. GR 924789.

Two short but fairly steep stretches, one uphill, the other down. Otherwise generally level walking.

Starting point The Windmill pub at Whiteley Green. Customers may leave their cars in the pub car park while they walk – but please ask the manager's permission. Otherwise park at the car park on the left just after the former railway bridge where our walk joins the Middlewood Way.

How to get there *The Windmill is on a byroad, Holehouse Lane, going east from the A523(T) 3½ miles north of Macclesfield town centre and 8 miles south of Stockport.*

Cheshire

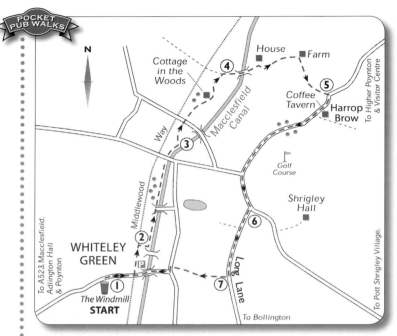

POCKET PUB WALKS

N

Cottage
in the Woods

House ■ ■ Farm

④

⑤

Coffee
Tavern ■ Harrop
Brow

To Higher Poynton
& Visitor Centre

Macclesfield Canal

Way

③

Golf
Course

Middlewood

Shrigley
Hall

②

⑥

WHITELEY
GREEN

To A523, Macclesfield,
Adlington Hall
& Poynton

Long Lane

The Windmill
START

①

⑦

To Pott Shrigley Village

To Bollington

1️⃣ From the **Windmill car park** turn right. On reaching the former railway bridge go down the steps, cross the plank bridge and turn left. After crossing the first bridge and by a sign for **Sugar Lane**, look for a stile on the right. Cross it and walk forward to follow a short green lane. Cross the stile and walk through the bracken to the canal towpath.

2️⃣ Turn left. Beyond the next bridge there is a pleasant wooded area to your left. After another bridge look for a stile on the left marked '**NCW**' (North Cheshire Way).

3️⃣ Cross the field, passing under the power lines to an oak tree and a stile in a dip. Cross this, turn right and, keeping the marshy ground to your left, head for another stile. Go across the lane and enter a drive. On reaching a garden gate, and the sight of a quaint timbered house hidden in the woods, cross the stile on the right and walk the overgrown path past a redundant stile. This will take you round the back of the house, where you should bear left over a peculiar makeshift stile and then continue left to a bridge. Cross it and walk up the bank, bearing right. Continue, aiming to the left of a bungalow to cross a stile. Turn left down the drive, and bear right at the fork.

4 Turn right onto a concrete road. Notice the sculpture on the right commemorating nearly 350 years of coal mining in the area. Cross the canal bridge and walk ahead past the caravan park. On reaching the gate to a house, pass between the fence and the post on the right and walk along a path between hedges. At its end turn left and cross the meadow to a stile just to the right of a farmhouse. Cross it, turn right and follow the hedge round to the left. Go through the kissing gate onto a sunken track, which will take you to a gate onto a lane.

The Coffee Tavern near Harrop Brow.

Cheshire

5 Turn right into the delightful hamlet of **Harrop Brow**. On the left is the **Coffee Tavern**, once public library, church and village hall, and now a café serving tea, coffee and delicious home-made cakes and selling local handicrafts. Go ahead at the junction. The lane becomes busier, so take care, but do enjoy the view over the old quarry and its pool towards **Alderley Edge**.

6 Turn right up **Long Lane**. This is something of a climb, but there is a seat if you need a rest. Ignore the first footpath sign on the right and continue along the lane, enjoying the ever-widening views. Looking to the left you will see the small town of **Bollington** and one of its old cotton mills. On the hill above the town is **White Nancy**, a curious monument to the victory at Waterloo in 1815.

7 As you go downhill, look for a stone stile on the right, almost hidden in the holly. Cross it and walk down the bank, keeping close to the hedgeside. Go through a hedge, and continue in the same direction to cross a stile onto a green lane. Cross another stile onto a lane by a former Primitive Methodist chapel. Turn left and immediately right and cross the canal bridge to return to your car.

Place of interest nearby

Adlington Hall has been the home of the Legh family since 1315. Part Tudor black and white and part Georgian brick, it contains an organ played by Handel. The house and its gardens with their maze are to the west of the A523(T) 1½ miles north of the Whiteley Green turn off and are open on Wednesdays in June, July and August.
☎ *01625 820875*

The Stamford Bridge

Stamford Bridge, 'the bridge at the stone ford',** lies on the old Roman road known in medieval times as Watling Street, which linked the legionary fortress at Chester with lesser forts at Northwich and Manchester, the salt mines of Middlewich and the industrial centre at Wilderspool (Warrington). Our walk takes us along part of the route of that road, but first we cross the fields to the village of Great Barrow, so close to the Roman road's successor, the very busy A51, yet with such an air of remoteness and peace that it would qualify as Cheshire's 'Shangri-la'. All around are wonderful views of the Cheshire and Welsh hills.

THE PUB The **Stamford Bridge** is a spacious, recently refurbished former coaching inn with pictures of Cheshire country houses on its walls. It has a large lawned beer garden with views of the open country where the adults can enjoy a pint of John Smith's, Timothy Taylor's or the current guest beer while the children amuse themselves in the play area. Fish features prominently on the menu, which includes poached salmon fillet, whole sea bass in crayfish sauce, and monkfish wrapped in Parma ham. There are also the usual steaks, curries and steak and kidney pie, while lighter meals include salmon and dill fishcakes, smoked haddock and crayfish sandwiches and a variety of toasted ciabattas.

Open from 11.30 am to 11 pm on Monday to Saturday and 12 noon to 10.30 pm on Sunday. Food is served from 12 noon to 9.30 pm on Monday to Saturday and 12 noon to 9 pm on Sunday.
☎ *01829 740229*

Distance – 2¾ miles.

OS Explorer 266 Wirral and Chester (with a very small section on 267 Northwich and Delamere Forest). GR 467674.

A pleasant stroll, suitable for all the family, across fields and along quiet lanes.

Starting point The Stamford Bridge pub. The pub car park is available to customers while they walk, with the permission of the management. Otherwise find a quiet spot in Lansdowne Road opposite.

How to get there *Stamford Bridge is on the B5132 close to its junction with the A51(T) 3¾ miles east of Chester city centre and 1½ miles west of Tarvin.*

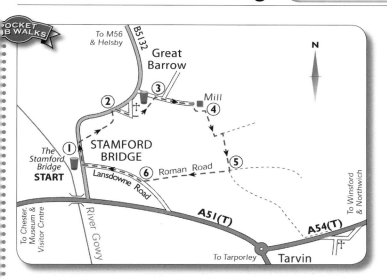

1. Turn left out of the car park of the **Stamford bridge pub** or right from **Lansdowne Road** and walk up the pavement of **Barrow Lane**, passing on the right **Greycot**, a cottage whose garden is scented with lilac, roses and honeysuckle in summer and has a very neatly clipped hedge. After passing a large bungalow go right, through a gate, into a field. Follow the hawthorn hedge on the right, keeping a line of young trees to your left. The path will become a green track between hedges with an orchard to its left. Cross the track of an abandoned miniature railway and head across the meadow towards the church tower. The large timbered house to its left is **Greysfield**, built in 1878 and subsequently much enlarged for a Liverpool grain merchant. Go left to cross a bridge and head for the metal gate at the end of the field.

2. Turn right onto the lane. Turn right again towards the church and then again to a gate with a superb view over the Cheshire countryside. The prominent hill ahead **is Larkton Hill** with its

prehistoric hill-fort **Maiden Castle**, while to the left are the **Peckforton Hills**. Do not go through the gate but turn left along the lawned path. You may wish to take a closer look at the church, which is open on Wednesdays from 10 am to 12.30 pm, when tea and coffee are served. Set in the perfect English churchyard with its yew and cedars and, of course, its view, its tower is mid 18th-century, its nave largely Victorian restoration and its chancel late 17th century, the gift of a dean of Chester. From the church gate continue in the same direction as before to pass through a gate onto a narrower path. To the left is the former vicarage with its Gothick windows.

3 On reaching the village street you will see the **White Horse pub** to the left, where, if you are in need of refreshment, you can have soup and sandwiches accompanied by Brakspear's Oxfordshire bitter. Otherwise turn right to pass a house of 1718 in a neat garden on your right and the village pump on your left. Proceed down **Mill Lane**. There is a timber-framed house to the left and then an old sandstone barn converted into a house. Cross the bridge and at **Mill House** bear right to pass the former mill and then left to see the millpond

4 Look for steps up to a gate on the right and walk down the left-hand side of the field. **Helsby and Overton (Frodsham) hills** can be glimpsed through a gap to the left. Cross a stile and plank bridge and turn left. Cross another plank bridge and stile and turn right. The 15th-century tower of **Tarvin church** can be seen ahead. Climb the ladder stile and walk along the right-hand edge of a large field with views of the **Clwydian hills** to the right. Cross a further stile and plank bridge and pause and look to your left. Here you will see **Eddisbury Hill**, which has another of Cheshire's hill-forts, occupied both in the Iron Age and by the Saxons.

5 Now turn right and walk along the right-hand edge of the field. You will probably notice that where you are walking is

slightly higher and drier than the rest of the field. This is because you are now walking on the Roman road. Make your way to a stile. Continue in the same direction with oaks for shade and a clump of woodland to your left. Cross a stile amongst hawthorns to walk along the right-hand edge of the next field – accompanied by lots of

St Bartholomew's church, Great Barrow.

butterflies and moths in summer. Cross a plank bridge and stile into a smaller field and then a stile followed by a plank bridge. Pass through a makeshift metal gate into sheep pasture and keep along its right-hand edge to a kissing gate in the corner.

6 Turn right into the lane, once the main road. You are soon back amongst the neat suburban-style gardens of **Stamford Bridge**. If you have not parked on the lane, bear left at its end for the pub, noting that it stands on the line of the old road, not the present one. If you care to walk on past it you will see the abutment of the old bridge at the stone ford.

Place of interest nearby

Chester Visitor Centre in Vicar's Lane overlooks Britain's largest Roman amphitheatre and contains finds made in the recent dig there. It is open every day except Christmas Day, Boxing Day and New Year's Day, and Roman soldier-led legionary tours start from it at 1.45 pm on Thursday to Saturday in June, July and August.
☎ *01244 402111*

10 Eaton-by-Tarporley

The Red Lion

Eaton is one of Cheshire's most picturesque villages, with a remarkable number of thatched cottages. This lovely walk takes us across fields, along quiet lanes, beside a golf course and through the village itself. With its wide views of the plain and the hills this is the sort of walk that would make an excellent introduction to the delights of Cheshire for someone who does not know the county.

THE PUB The **Red Lion**, which is the 20th-century replacement for a much older inn, has lovely views of the countryside from the tables in its forecourt. It also has a children's playground and what is now a rarity amongst pub facilities, a bowling green. The beers on draught are Morland Old Speckled Hen, Wells Bombardier and Mann's Chestnut Mild. The lunchtime bar menu

Distance – 3½ miles.

OS Explorer 267 Northwich and Delamere Forest. GR 575637.

Easy walking over a gently undulating countryside.

Starting point The Red Lion in Eaton. Customers may leave their cars in the pub car park while they walk – but do ask the licensee's permission. Otherwise find a quiet spot in Eaton village and walk down the lane to the pub.

How to get there The Red Lion can be reached easily from the A49 Warrington to Whitchurch road by turning into Eaton Lane by the Cotebrook Shire Horse Centre.

includes the fish of the day in beer batter, steak and Guinness pie and bangers and mash, while in the evening you can order lamb Henry, roast loin of pork or lamb cutlets, or choose from a variety of fish and chicken dishes.

Open from 5 pm to 11 pm on Monday, 12 noon to 3 pm and 5 pm to 11 pm on Tuesday, Wednesday and Thursday, 12 noon to 11 pm on Friday and Saturday and 12 noon to 10.30 pm on Sunday. Food is served from 6 pm to 8.30 pm on Monday and Saturday, 12 noon to 2.30 pm and 6 pm to 8.30 pm on Tuesday to Friday and 12 noon to 7 pm on Sunday.
☎ *01829 732263*

1 From the **Red Lion** car park, turn left into the lane, walk past the former Wesleyan chapel and find a path on the right, parallel with the road. Climb the steps to a gate and cross the small field to another. Walk forward across a much bigger field, keeping

the copse to your left. As you reach a hedge, look back and enjoy the attractive wooded landscape. Cross a stile and a short, decayed plank bridge, and head towards a farm.

2 On reaching the farm buildings turn right to pass in front of the farmhouse. Ignore the footpath sign and carry on along the lane. Notice the dry sandstone walls with hawthorn hedges growing on top of them. These are a feature of the lanes around Eaton and are called cops.

3 At the T-junction, where there is a Victorian post box in the wall, turn right. Ignore the stiles and continue along the lane, where there are far-reaching views from a gate on the left. Do not cross the stile on the left, though it is worth pausing again for the view. Go straight across the next T-junction to a stile and walk up the path ahead over the field. Cross the next stile and follow

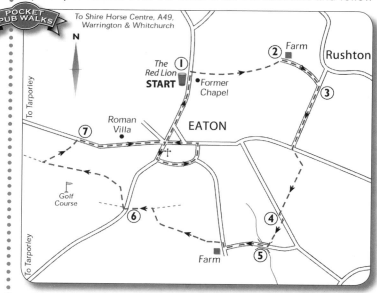

The church of St Thomas, Eaton.

the line of trees, aiming for a metal gate at the far end of the hedge on your right.

4 Turn left into the lane and then cross a stile on your right. Go over the field to a stile near the far left corner. There will probably be an electric fence on the left when you have crossed the stile. Take care not to touch it and make your way to a stile beneath a large oak.

5 Turn right into a lane where you will hear the pleasant sound of running water from an unseen stream. At the end of the lane turn right, pass the farm buildings and then go left through a gate into a field. Having passed the house on your left, look out across the sheep pasture for medieval **Beeston Castle** on its bluff. Cross the stile and aim for the far right-hand corner of the big field. Cross the stile here and walk along the right-hand edge of the meadow to another stile.

6 Cross the busy road with care to enter a golf course at the footpath sign. The path marked on the OS map goes straight uphill here but it is sensible to avoid flying golf balls by following the new path along the right-hand edge of the course. At the top of the rise, where the path becomes surfaced, look back for a long view over the Cheshire plain. On reaching a large holly tree look for a path to a stile on the right by a gate, and walk down a shady green lane.

7 On reaching a road, turn right and head into **Eaton village**. In the grounds of the first house on the left are the remains of a Roman villa. Enjoy the lovely old houses as you approach the village cross, a replacement for one destroyed by the Puritans. Turn right here to pass the neat little late-Victorian **church of St Thomas** and, just beyond it on the left, **Bay Tree**, a rare example in these parts of the traditional longhouse, where people and livestock lived under one roof. Now turn left into **Edgewell Lane** with its timbered and thatched cottages. Turn left at the junction and walk on the pavement. At a small green turn left again. Having passed a junction, on the right you will see a door at the foot of a vertical bank. This hides what was once the village well. Turn right and, having passed the former smithy on the right, head up the lane back to the **Red Lion**.

Place of interest nearby

Cotebrook Shire Horse Centre and Countryside Park is on the A49 only a mile from the Red Lion. In addition to the horses, there are miniature ponies, pigs, goats, ducks, hens, foxes, red deer, red squirrels and birds of prey, as well as a nature trail, picnic area and gift shop. Open every day from 10 am to 5 pm.
☎ *01829 760506*

11 Goostrey

The Red Lion

Goostrey is a village famous in the county for its annual gooseberry show. From it we walk across the fields and through the woods of mid-Cheshire's dairying country to discover a tiny cruck cottage, a 16th-century farmhouse, an old watermill and a 1,200-year-old tree, all almost within the shadow of a 20th-century radio telescope.

THE PUB
The **Red Lion** is a 17th-century former coaching house with a ghost called Pandora. It is a very walker-friendly inn. Telephone ahead and sandwiches will be prepared for you to take on your walk or there will be a meal ready on your return, while in winter a cosy fire will be lit to greet you. There is a games room with table football, pinball and a vintage jukebox, and a comfortable bar and restaurant. The menu usually includes

an excellent home-made soup, a roast, various omelettes and a vegetarian dish such as roast vegetable tagliatelle or mushroom stroganoff, plus a hot pudding like damson tart and custard. An all-day breakfast is also available. The beers served include Tetley's and Archer's Bad Trousers.

Open from 11 am to 11 pm on Monday to Saturday and 12 noon to 10.30 pm on Sunday. Food is served from 12 noon to 2 pm and 6.30 pm to 9 pm on Monday to Saturday, 12 noon to 3 pm and 5.30 pm to 7 pm on Sunday and at other times by special request.
☎ *01477 532033*

1 From the **Red Lion car park** turn right. On your right you will see a deep dell which in the early Middle Ages was a moat

Distance – 4 miles.

OS Explorer 268 Wilmslow, Macclesfield and Congleton. GR 779699.

Easy, level walking suitable for all ages.

Starting point The Red Lion near Goostrey's church. The pub car park may be used by customers – after asking permission – while they are on the walk.

How to get there *The Red Lion is reached via Goostrey Lane, which is west of the A535 Alderley Edge road 2½ miles north of the centre of Holmes Chapel and 3¾ miles from junction 18 of the M6. If you prefer the train, the pub is about 3 minutes walk from Goostrey station on the Manchester Piccadilly–Crewe line.*

protecting a house which stood where the church is now. Look for a footpath sign across the road and go up the steps. Pass through a gate and walk along a path between a holly hedge and a fence. Go left alongside the cemetery. Beyond the footpath that bisects it and on its own is a mass grave containing remains taken from the church vaults when the coffins began to collapse. Go through

The charming Hawthorne Cottage.

the gate and follow the hedge round to the right. Walk between a school on the right and a paddock on the left. Beyond the next gate turn left and walk along the left-hand edge of the field. Cross the stile and go ahead across a large field, aiming for a tall post. The official footpath appears to be on the other side of the stile here, but nettles, brambles, barbed wire and a steep slope make it almost impossible to walk. You should therefore turn left and walk along the field edge to a gate. Before you pass through it look left and you will have a good view of the **Jodrell Bank telescope**. Beyond the gate go down the steps, cross the bridge over the brook and walk alongside the large hawthorn hedge to your right.

2 Cross a stile and turn right onto a lane. It is very quiet but take care on the bends. This is dairying country, and **Orchards Farm** on the left has the appearance of a model farm. Ignore the footpath sign on the right here and continue along the lane until you come to a paddock with donkeys and miniature ponies.

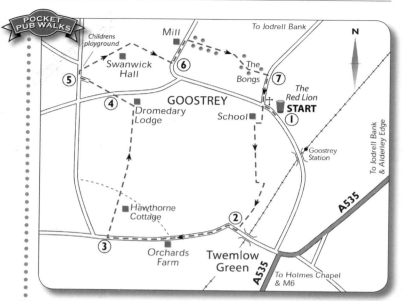

3 Turn right and go through a gate onto a drive. You will pass the tiny, timbered **Hawthorne Cottage** on your right. Notice the pheasant in its thatch. Go slightly right along an oak-shaded track between a ditch and a field. You will reach a crossroads of paths. You should go ahead through the gate and cross a very large field. Walk along the left-hand side of a line of sycamores and oaks to another gate. Continue ahead, with a paddock to your right, onto a grassy area and go through a gate. Keeping the house, the oddly named **Dromedary Lodge**, on your right, aim to the left of the barn conversion and go forward down the drive.

4 On reaching the road, cross to the pavement and turn left. Turn right up an unmade road, **Sandy Lane**, keeping right at the junction. At the end of the road is a small green.

5 Turn right and then right again by the children's playground and

go along a metalled track to pass the late 16th-century **Swanwick Hall** on your right. Go through two gates and turn right to walk alongside a hedge. Pass through a gate onto a board-walk and then through another gate to walk along the right-hand edge of a field. Go ahead to a choice of stile, gate or gap, and cross the next field on a well-defined path. Passing a pond on your right you will reach a gate.

6 Turn left onto the lane. You will pass a former water-driven corn-mill with its hoist on your left. Cross the bridge and turn right onto a wooded path. Cross the footbridge and go up the steps and through a kissing gate to walk along the right-hand edge of a meadow with a steep slope to your right. Go down some steps and through another kissing gate to re-enter the wood. Cross a stream and head up a bank with holly and oaks. Cross a bridge and walk ahead to a gate to the left of the garage of the white house. Note that there is a hook as well as a latch on the gate.

7 Turn right into the lane and walk along the verge or pavement towards **Goostrey church**. As you pass its tower, look left and you will see the 1,200-year-old yew tree. Turn left at the war memorial to return to the **Red Lion**.

Place of interest nearby

Jodrell Bank, 2 miles from Goostrey, is home to the famous Lovell radio telescope (now a grade 1 listed building), an environmental discovery centre and an arboretum. Reached via the A535, it is open from mid-March to October between 10.30 am and 5.30 pm every day. From November to mid-March it is open from 10.30 am to 3 pm on weekdays and 11 am to 4 pm at the weekend.
☎ 01477 571339

12 **Sutton Lane Ends**

The Church House

Sutton means the village to the south of the town (of Macclesfield). Lane Ends refers to the fact that the decent roads used to end here where the plain meets the Pennine hills. We walk along the slopes of one of those hills and enjoy ever-changing views of some of the others and across the plain, having first encountered what is perhaps the most interesting section of the Macclesfield Canal.

THE PUB The **Church House** is a comfortable early-Victorian pub with a beer garden and a play area. The beers are Boddington's and Robinson's, plus changing guest ales. The menu includes chilli and lime pork sausages and mash, Penang chicken, spinach, ricotta and goat's cheese cannelloni and, for those with less exotic tastes, farmhouse grill, liver and onions, steak and ale pie and bubble battered cod with chips and mushy peas. There are also sandwiches, toasties and baguettes.

Open from 12 noon to 3 pm and 5 pm to 11 pm on Monday to Friday, 12 noon to 11 pm on Saturday and 12 noon to 10.30 pm on Sunday. Food is served from 12 noon to 2 pm and 5 pm to 9 pm on Monday to Friday and 12 noon to 9.30 pm on Saturday and Sunday.
☎ *01260 252436*

1 From the **Church House car park** turn left and walk along the pavement. You will soon come to an attractive group of early-Victorian buildings – church, school and vicarage, all erected in the 1840s. Bear right at the junction and cross the bridge. There

Distance – 3½ miles.

OS Explorer 268 Wilmslow, Macclesfield and Congleton. GR 931713.

Some uphill sections but the spectacular views repay the effort. This is an excellent introduction to Pennine Cheshire.

Starting point The Church House pub in Church Lane, Sutton Lane Ends. The pub car park is available for customers while they are walking, but please ask permission first. Otherwise park in the lay-by alongside the canal in Bullocks Lane (off Byron's Lane) and start the walk just beyond point 3.

How to get there The Church House is reached via Byron's Lane and Jarman Lane from the Sutton, Langley and Wincle signpost on the east side of the A523 Leek road about ¾ mile south of Macclesfield town centre.

is a dangerous bend ahead so cross to the pavement, which is now on the other side of the road. To the right is **Church View Terrace**, still with some of its original Victorian door-cases.

2 Turn right at the crossroads and then left into a footpath just before the bridge. The path with its shrubs seems to be an extension of the garden across the stream, where there are always lots of ducks. Cross over the stile and aim for the far right-hand corner of the sheep pasture, where there is a stile onto a farm track.

3 At the track's end turn right to pass the end of the drive to **Sutton Hall**. Go over the canal bridge and at the lay-by turn right and left onto the towpath. As you cross the aqueduct over the **river Bollin**, look to the right. The small stone building next to the white house is where the great canal engineer James Brindley was apprenticed to a millwright. The high retaining walls on both banks are very impressive. Notice the milestone just before **bridge 43**, which was specially constructed to enable a barge-horse to cross from one towpath to the other without being

Bridge number 43.

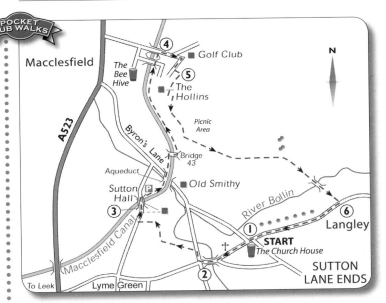

unhitched. The prominent church spire ahead as we leave the cutting belongs to **St Paul's, Macclesfield**, built in the 1840s. Nearer to hand is the tower of **St Peter's, Sutton**, which was built around the same time. Just beyond the second bridge after the **Bee Hive pub**, which is sadly on the opposite bank, you will see a bench. Here turn right up the steps to reach a lane.

4️⃣ Turn left and walk uphill, keeping right at the junction. Here are some attractive cottages from Macclesfield's heyday as a silk manufacturing town. Turn right at the golf club gates and walk along a stony track. There is an excellent view of **Macclesfield** over the wall to the right.

5️⃣ Go up the steps in the wall on the left onto a narrow path. On reaching a field the path bends to the left and becomes quite shady. Where it forks do not go right, onto the golf course, but bear left uphill. Cross a stony lane and go ahead to some picnic tables. The hills you can see from here are, from the left, **Sutton Common** with its mast, **Gawsworth Common** and **Bosley Cloud**. Now head up the stony track and, having passed an underground reservoir, turn right onto a narrow path amongst the gorse. Go through a metal kissing gate and head uphill. As the main track appears to swing left, go slightly right through a hedge of small trees into the next field, where the track is well defined. The hill coming into view on the left is **Tegg's Nose**, now a country park, with its outlier, **Ward's Knob**. Walk towards it and go through a gap in the hedge by a holly bush. Follow the most obvious of the paths here, which goes slightly right, and pass through the left-hand of the two gaps in the overgrown hedge, the other being boggy. Turn right and head towards a metal kissing gate. Beyond it a track is discernible towards the left; this is briefly like a sunken green lane. Follow it towards a prominent split sycamore and cross the footbridge over the **Bollin**. Now walk left up the sheep pasture and then alongside a high stone wall to a stile onto a road.

6 You are now in the curiously suburban outskirts of the Pennine village of **Langley**. Turn right and walk along the pavement, back to the **Church House**.

Place of interest nearby

The **Heritage Centre**, Roe Street, Macclesfield, which is housed in an impressive Sunday School building erected in 1814, contains a gallery devoted to the history of silk manufacture in the town, with an excellent display of costume from the 1830s to the present day. Open from 11 am to 5 pm on Monday to Saturday and 12 noon to 4.30 pm on Sunday.
☎ *01625 613210*

13 **Astbury**

The Egerton Arms

Astbury's village green, hedged about with lovely old houses and overlooked by a grand medieval church, is one the most photographed places in Cheshire. Less well known but equally delightful is Astbury Mere, and we walk beside this before heading along ancient hollow-ways or sunken lanes to the market town of Congleton and its unspoiled Georgian church. From there we walk across a golf course, along a canal towpath and down a country lane to see a hilltop folly and the site of a medieval manor house.

THE PUB The **Egerton Arms** was built in 1560 and is the sort of place where you might expect to see a ghost, and it is indeed said to be haunted, by a woman in white, murdered by her husband in the house next door. This is, however, an attractive, walker-friendly hostelry with a children's

Distance – 4 miles.

OS Explorer 268 Wilmslow, Macclesfield and Congleton. GR 846615.

Some steep steps to climb but this is a very rewarding walk. Be prepared for traffic on the lanes at times.

Starting point The Egerton Arms in Astbury. Customers may leave their cars in the pub car park while they are walking but should ask permission first. Otherwise find a spot on the green.

How to get there The Egerton Arms is accessible from the A34 Congleton to Newcastle-under-Lyme road a mile south of its junctions with the A54 and A534

play area and a bright and cheerful restaurant. On the menu are roast local turkey with sage, parsley and thyme stuffing, crispy roast duckling with orange and ginger sauce, cranberry baked ham and vegetable stroganoff. The beers available are Unicorn and Double Hop from Robinson's Stockport brewery and Hartley's XB.

Open from 11.30 am to 11 pm on Monday to Saturday and 11.30 am to 3 pm and 6.45 pm to 10.30 pm on Sunday. Food is served from 11.30 am to 2 pm and 6.30 pm to 9 pm on Monday to Saturday; 12 noon to 2 pm and 6.45 pm to 9 pm on Sunday.
☎ *01260 273946*

1 Walk from the **Egerton Arms car park** in the direction of the church tower and turn right towards the village green. On reaching the main road, turn right and then cross the road with

care into **Bent Lane**. Here go immediately right to a stile and walk along the path through the field. Go diagonally right across the next field to another stile. Turn right onto a path between houses, left onto a road and right at the junction.

2 Having re-crossed the main road go through the green gate ahead. Go ahead through the gate to walk past **Astbury Sail Sports**. At the end of its car park, walk on beside the seaside-like sandy shore of the lake. Just beyond the green metal fence, turn right into the country park and go up the steps made of railway sleepers. At the junction of paths turn right and go up some more steps. Walk

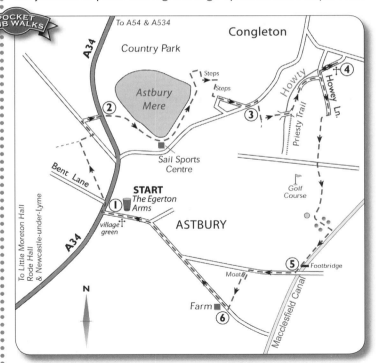

along a path, looking for further steps on the right. Climb them and at the top ignore the first path on the left and turn left at a T-junction of paths to walk alongside a green onto the road ahead.

The 17th-century gateway to Astbury churchyard.

3. Turn left at the junction. Look out for a sign for **Astbury village** on the right and turn into an old sunken path. Beyond a large oak go left over a stile at the sign for **Congleton** and follow the hawthorn hedge along another sunken path. Cross a stile and walk across the meadow to a bridge over a stream called the **Howty**. Go left briefly but look for a gate to your right. Pass through it and turn left to follow the stream to a gate onto a lane. At the end of the lane, turn left into **Moody Street**. Turn right towards **Congleton church** and call at the vicarage next door for the key and enjoy the church's unspoilt Georgian interior.

4. From the church retrace your steps to the junction and turn left to ascend **Howey Lane**. At its top take the path on the right. Go through the gate and take the well-defined path across the meadow. Go through the metal gate and cross a track. Follow the shaded path alongside the paddock and then keep ahead across the golf course, noticing the water tower on the left. Follow the line of oaks and at their end go right and then left onto a path

between smaller oaks to a further part of the course. Again follow the trees. Head briefly towards a pond and then turn left into a wood. Continue on the broad path ahead and turn right to walk along the towpath of the **Macclesfield Canal**.

5 When you reach a path on the right between a footbridge and a road bridge, take it and turn right into the lane. Look out for a footpath sign by the first house on the left. Walk through the garden. The pond to the right is a remnant of the moat of a vanished medieval house, **Newbold Manor**. Go over the stile and bear right along the perimeter of the meadow. Towards the left is **Mow Cop** with its mock ruined castle, built in 1754 to enhance the view from **Rode Hall**.

6 Cross the stile and turn right into the lane, passing **Meadow Bank Farm** on the left. Go left at the junction. This road can be busy, so walk along the verge and pavement until the latter's end, where you should cross to the one on the other side. As you approach **Astbury church** notice how the tower appears to be detached. The church is open on Sundays and bank holidays from 2 pm to 5 pm, when tea and cakes are served. The entrance to the **Egerton Arms car park** is almost immediately on your right.

Place of interest nearby

Little Moreton Hall is perhaps the most famous of Cheshire's timbered houses. Built between 1480 and 1559 and owned by the National Trust, it is 2 miles south of Astbury on the A34. Noted for its spectacular long gallery and its wall paintings, it also has a knot garden. Open 11.30 am to 5 pm on Wednesday to Monday from March to October and 11.30 am to 4.30 pm on Saturday and Sunday in November and early December.
☎ *01260 272018*

The Swan Inn

Wybunbury (pronounced 'Winbury')** is built on salt. Underground springs have caused this to subside in places. Consequently the church has had to be demolished, leaving its magnificent medieval tower standing alone in the churchyard. As remarkable as Wybunbury's leaning tower is its Moss. Here subsidence has created a 40 ft deep lake topped by a 3 ft layer of sphagnum moss-covered peat. Now a nature reserve, this rare floating bog is home to many rare species of plant and animal life. On this walk we see both tower and Moss, as well as the site of a medieval bishop's house.

THE PUB

The **Swan Inn** is the ideal Cheshire village inn. Dating from the 15th century it offers well-kept Jennings ales plus two guest beers and a wide range of well-cooked food served in generous portions. There are also six en-suite bedrooms, making it a first class base for a walking holiday in the county.

The special two course lunch offers a good home-made soup plus the old pub favourites, gammon, steak and ale pie and fish and chips and a vegetarian dish. Sandwiches include baked ham and mustard, gravadlax with dill dressing and roast chicken and cranberry. In the evening the most popular starter seems to be the famous Swan fishcake, while main courses include crispy roast duckling with apple and sultana compote, glazed shoulder of lamb, Indian spiced chicken breast and beef fillet stroganoff.

Open from 11.30 am to 11 pm on Tuesday to Sunday and 5 pm to 11 pm on Monday. Food is served from 6 pm to 9.30 pm on Monday, 12 noon to 2 pm and 6 pm to 9.30 pm on Tuesday to Saturday and 12 noon to 8 pm on Sunday.
☎ *01270 841280*

Distance – 4 miles.

OS Explorer 257 Crewe and Nantwich. GR 699498.

Largely level, easy walking. The ground can be boggy in places, so make sure you are appropriately shod.

Starting point The Swan Inn at the east end of Wybunbury. Customers may leave their cars in the Swan's car park while they walk, but should obtain the management's permission first. Otherwise, use the car park next to the new church and children's playground (open 9 am to 8 pm, or dusk if earlier) and start the walk at point 2.

How to get there *Wybunbury lies between the A500(T) Nantwich to Newcastle-under-Lyme and A51 Nantwich to Stone roads. It is signposted from both roads a mile or so east of Nantwich town centre.*

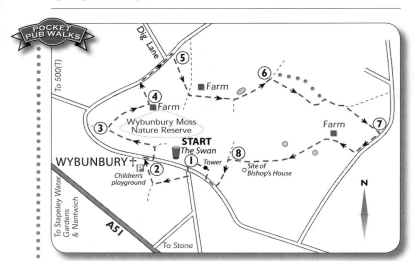

POCKET PUB WALKS

1 From the pub car park turn left and pass the 18th-century **Red Lion** on your right. Opposite **Wrinehill Road** turn right up an unmade track between the houses. On reaching a meadow, continue ahead to follow a row of trees on its right-hand edge, where you will see a faint path. Follow the hedge round to the right to cross a stile. Climb the bank and walk up the right-hand edge of the playing field. Pass the children's playground and the car park on your left and walk on to the village street.

2 Go right to pass the village hall and turn left up **Kiln Lane**, an unmade track. Where this swings right, cross the stile on the left. Walk on to another stile and then along the left-hand edge of a meadow to a stile beneath a holly tree. Continue ahead across a meadow, which seems to serve as a lawn to the house you are approaching. Keeping the house on your right, go straight ahead along its drive to a footpath sign. This will point you into a tunnel of young trees. At its end go through a gate onto a path alongside a wire fence. Wybunbury Moss is on your right.

3 At a gate by a wooden pinfold turn right onto a stony lane. Approach a farm (a rare breeds centre) and pass through the gap by the gate, keeping the farmhouse on your right.

4 Go up the steps on the left here to walk between an arable field and a paddock. Cross a stile and walk alongside a hawthorn hedge to a lane. Cross to the pavement on the other side and turn right.

5 On reaching **Dig Lane** re-cross the road to a metal kissing gate. Go over the meadow to a stile in a hedge and then follow a well-defined path across the next field, where there is a line of poplars on the left. Cross a stile, a farm lane and another stile. Go left along the field edge, ignoring the arrow pointing towards Wybunbury tower. Cross the stile by the farmhouse and then another stile into a paddock. Keep along its left-hand edge to a further stile, which you will notice has been well bitten by horses. Cross it and go forward to the corner of this paddock, where you should turn right and cross a stile to walk alongside a large fishpond or reservoir with willows and often moorhens. At the pond's end go ahead across the meadow, aiming for the left-hand edge of a copse.

The church tower without its church, Wybunbury.

Cheshire

6 Do not go through the gate here but turn right to walk along the left-hand edge of the field. Cross the stile by the second 'Danger snakes' sign (you are more likely to see woodpeckers and nuthatches here than snakes). Go left and follow the edge of the big field to a stile under a large oak. Cross this and walk along the left-hand edge of the meadow to a stile level with some farm buildings on your right. Cross it and continue along the edge of the field. Faced with a choice of stiles, take the one on the right and walk towards the road.

7 Do not cross the stile onto the road but turn right and walk along the field's edge until you reach a farm track. Turn right here and head towards the farmhouse. On reaching it, cross the stile and walk across the rather boggy meadow to another stile to the right of a pond. Cross it and aim towards the tower. Cross a stile in a hawthorn hedge. Continue to another stile in a hedge and head across a large field, aiming just to the right of the left-hand tree (an oak). Walk along the left-hand edge of the next field. On your left, with its dry moat, is the site of the house of the medieval bishops of Lichfield. At the end of the field turn right and then left to a stile.

8 Turn left onto a track and follow it to its end. Turn right into the lane by the very impressive former vicarage and go up the steps on the right for a closer look at the tower. Now walk the short distance back to the **Swan Inn**.

Place of interest nearby

Stapeley Water Gardens, 2 miles north-west of Wybunbury on the A51, are the home of the National Collection of Water Lilies. There is also a 'tropical oasis' with sharks, stingrays and monkeys. Open daily except Christmas Day. ☎ *01270 623868*

15 Grindley Brook

The Horse and Jockey

Grindley Brook is just on the Shropshire side of the county boundary. This walk takes us along the towpath of the Llangollen branch of the Shropshire Union Canal and then along a quiet lane to the hidden Cheshire hamlet of Wirswall. This tiny place was once a medieval borough and market town, which failed probably because of its position amongst the hills and its proximity to the Shropshire town of Whitchurch. As we return to Grindley Brook by ancient sunken lanes we enjoy some good views over the Welsh and Shropshire countryside.

THE PUB The **Horse and Jockey** is a former coaching house with friendly staff and a friendly ghost. It has a patio and a play area, and generous helpings of simple but well-cooked pub food can be enjoyed in the comfortable bar. Peppered pork, liver and onions, steak and ale pie, lasagne and a huge mixed

Distance – 4½ miles.

OS Explorer 257 Crewe and Nantwich. GR 522432.

The walk does entail a steady climb up to Wirswall and a long descent, but it is not difficult.

Starting point The Horse and Jockey in Grindley Brook. Customers may leave their cars in the pub car park while walking – but do ask the licensee's permission.

How to get there The Horse and Jockey is at the junction of the A41 Chester road and the B5395 to Malpas ½ mile north-west of the Whitchurch bypass (A49).

grill are the staples of the menu. The generous puddings include sherry trifle, toffee cheesecake and chocolate fudge cake. Sandwiches and baguettes are also available and can be washed down with a pint of Greene King IPA or one of the guest beers.

Open from 12 noon to 3 pm and 5 pm to 11 pm on Monday to Friday and 12 noon to 11 pm on Saturday and Sunday. Food is served from 12 noon to 2.30 pm on Monday to Friday, 12 noon to 9 pm on Saturday and 12 noon to 8.30 pm on Sunday.
☎ *01948 662723*

1 From the pub car park cross the road and walk up the left-hand side of the petrol station, noticing the tiny brook at the bottom of the cottage garden on the left. At **Honeysuckle Cottage** turn left onto the canal towpath and pass under the bridge. You are now in Cheshire. Look out for the **Sandstone Trail** sign on the left as you approach **Willeymoor Lock** and the former lock-keeper's cottage, now expanded into a pub.

Turn right and cross over the lock and the bridge over the canal overflow, then a ditch and stile to walk along the path parallel to the pub drive. After a further stile, cross the main road with care and go right and left into **Bradeley Green Lane**. At the house at the top of the lane ignore the footpath signs to the right and go ahead along a green lane. Where the wooded area ends go through the gate and walk up the cart track ahead. At the **Bishop Bennet Way** sign, go left through the gate, and turn right to pass in front of **The Spinney**, and then right again onto a lane. Pass **Wirswall Hall** on the right and, after the **Grange** and just before a bungalow, turn right onto a bridleway.

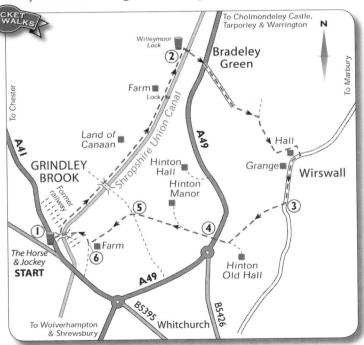

Cheshire

3 At a stile the path becomes a sunken way with long views ahead into Wales. Go over a cross track to a gate marked '**SCW**' for South Cheshire Way, although you are in fact re-entering Shropshire. Walk on between two barbed wire fences onto a track which becomes neatly mown as it passes a timber-framed house. Walk down the drive away from the house to the A49 and take care as you cross it.

4 Enter the lane ahead with its views over Shropshire to the left. Pass some houses and cross over a cattle grid onto pasture with more fine views. Do not follow the main drive to **Hinton Manor**, but go slightly left towards a gate and an avenue of trees. Here bear right into what becomes a sunken lane.

5 Take the middle one of three gates and walk along the left-hand side of a meadow. Ignore the stile to your left and keep ahead uphill. A path is now just about discernible. Go through the metal gate and walk along the edge of the field to a stile in front of the farmhouse. Cross this into another field and bear right to a gate in its far left-hand corner.

6 Turn right onto a lane and pass under a most impressive railway bridge. From here carry on over the canal bridge back to the **Horse and Jockey**.

Place of interest nearby

Cholmondeley Castle Garden is on the A49 about 7 miles north of Grindley Brook. In addition to the extensive ornamental gardens dominated by a romantic Gothick castle there is a children's corner with animals and a play area. Open Good Friday to late September on Sundays, Wednesdays, Thursdays and bank holidays from 11.30 am to 5 pm. ☎ *01829 720383*